Reptiles

KINGFISHER

First published 2006 by Kingfisher

This edition published 2008 by Kingfisher
an imprint of Macmillan Children's Books
a division of Macmillan Publishers Limited
20 New Wharf Road, London N1 9RR
Basingstoke and Oxford
www.panmacmillan.com

Associated companies throughout the world

ISBN 978-0-7534-1371-5

Acknowledgements
The publisher would like to thank the following for permission to reproduce their material. Every care has been taken
to trace copyright holders. However, if there have been unintentional omissions or failure to trace copyright holders,
we apologise and will, if informed, endeavour to make corrections in any future edition.
b = bottom, c = centre, l = left, t = top, r = right

Photographs: cover Ingo Arndt/Naturepl.com; 1bc Alamy/FLPA/Chris Mattison; 3bc Jurgen & Christine Sohns/FLPA; 4–5c Corbis/Rod Patterson;
6–7bl Getty Images/Marvin E. Newman; 7t Getty Images/Jeffrey L. Rotman; 7crb Kingfisher/Art Bank; 8b Photolibrary.com/OSF/Tui De Roy;
9tr Photolibrary.com/OSF/Mark Hamblin; 9cl Corbis/Frank Lukasseck; 9br Photolibrary.com/OSF/Robin Bush; 10cl NHPA/Daniel Heuclin;
10–11cl Corbis/Michael & Patricia Fogden; 11br Cyril Ruoso/JH Editorial/Minden Pictures/FLPA; 12bl Getty Images/Richard Coomber; 12–13t Yossi
Eshbol/FLPA; 13b Heidi & Hans-Juergen Koch/Minden Pictures/FLPA; 14bl John Cancalosi/Naturepl.com; 15t Corbis/George McCarthy; 15bl David
Kjaer/Naturepl.com; 16b Corbis/John Conrad; 17t Getty Images/Peter Weber; 17cr Getty Images/Dr Dennis Kunkel; 17b Corbis/Joe McDonald;
18bl Photolibrary.com/OSF; 19tr Barry Mansell/Naturepl.com; 19br Anup Shah/Naturepl.com; 20b Corbis/Nigel J. Dennis; 21t Getty Images/Paul
Chesley; 21cl Corbis/ Michael & Patricia Fogden; 21c Alamy/IT Stock Free/Dynamics Graphics Group; 22bl Tui De Roy/Minden Pictures/FLPA; 23cl Flip
Nicklin/Minden Pictures/FLPA; 23b Photolibrary.com/OSF/Tobias Bernhard; 24c Pete Oxford/Minden Pictures/FLPA; 25tr Photolibrary.com/OSF/Stan
Osolinski; 25cl NHPA/Stephen Dalton; 25br NHPA/Stephen Dalton; 26c Photolibrary.com/OSF/Ingo Arndt; 27tl Patricia & Michael Fogden/Minden
Pictures/FLPA; 27cr NHPA/Daniel Heuclin; 27br Photolibrary.com/OSF/Michael Fogden; 28b Photolibrary.com/OSF/Michael Fogden; 29cl D. Zingel
Eichhorn/FLPA; 29cr Rupert Barrington/Naturepl.com; 30b Michael & Patricia Fogden/Minden Pictures/FLPA; 31tr Getty Images/Steve Winter; 31br
NHPA/Laurie Campbell; 32b Getty Images/Bill Curtsinger; 33tl Chris Mattison/FLPA; 33cr NHPA/Martin Harvey; 34–35bc Corbis/Rod Patterson; 35tr
Getty Images/Altrendo Nature; 35br Getty Images/Theo Allofs; 36bl John Cancalosi/Naturepl.com; 37tr Photolibrary.com/OSF/Dani Jeske; 37b Getty
Images/Theo Allofs; 38bl NHPA/Anthony Bannister; 38–39c Photolibrary.com/OSF/Tobias Bernhard; 39tr ZSSD/Minden Pictures/FLPA; 39br Getty
Images/Joel Sartore; 40cl NHPA/Daniel Heuclin; 40br Still Pictures/Lynda Richardson; 40–41c Corbis/Philip Gould; 48br Getty Images/Jeff Hunter.

Commissioned photography on pages 42–47 by Andy Crawford
Project-maker and photoshoot co-ordinator: Jo Connor
Thank you to models Dilvinder Dilan Bhamra, Cherelle Clarke, Madeleine Roffey and William Sartin

Kingfisher Young Knowledge

Reptiles

Belinda Weber

Contents

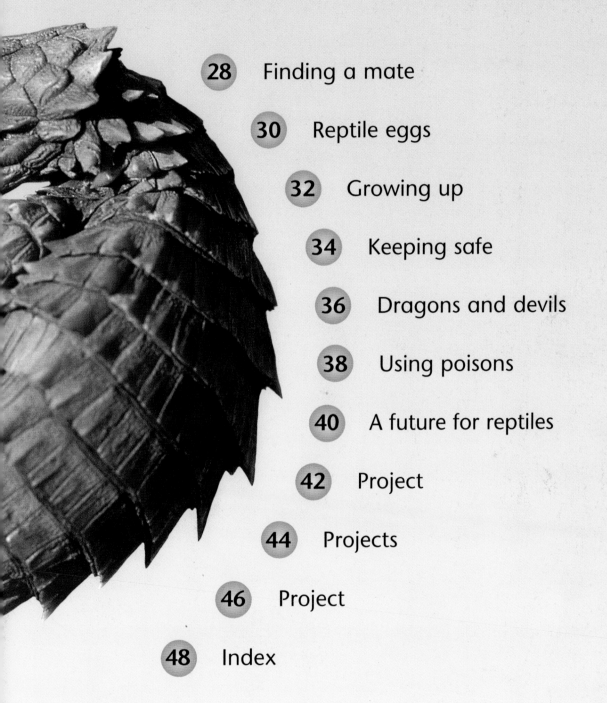

What is a reptile?

Reptiles are a group of animals with tough, scaly skin. They have a skeleton and backbone. There are more than 6,500 different kinds of reptiles.

Tough and scaly

Reptile skin is covered in thin, protective plates called scales, stronger than normal skin. Alligators have skin covered in thick, horny plates.

skeleton – *a frame of bones inside an animal's body*

7

Water features

Crocodiles live near water. Like water birds, they have webbed feet to help them swim.

Different homes

All reptiles are suited to where they live. Alligators have a body for moving both in and out of water.

Prehistoric reptiles

Reptiles have prehistoric ancestors. Archelon was a giant sea reptile related to modern-day turtles.

ancestor – an animal from which later animals have developed

Different types

Reptiles come in many shapes and sizes. Largest of all are the saltwater crocodiles, which grow to about seven metres long. Reptiles can be placed into four different groups.

Reptiles with shells

Turtles, terrapins and tortoises belong to this group. They all have hard, bony shells to protect the soft body inside.

species – *a set of animals or plants with the same features*

Lizards and snakes

This is the largest reptile group. There are more than 3,000 different species of lizards and snakes found all over the world.

The crocodilians

Alligators, crocodiles, caimans and gharials belong to this group. They can all move quickly over land, but most are found wallowing in water.

A group apart

Tuataras are the only members of the smallest reptile group. They are only found on a few small islands off the coast of New Zealand.

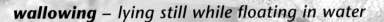

wallowing – lying still while floating in water

Temperature control

Reptiles are cold-blooded, which means their bodies stay at the same temperature as their surroundings. They lie in the sun to warm up and hide in the shade to cool down. Once warm, they hunt for food.

Too cool to move

When some reptiles, such as rattlesnakes, find it too cold, they hibernate (go into a deep sleep) until warmer weather returns.

digest – *to break down food so that the body can use it*

Keeping warm
Chameleons bask in the sun to heat up their blood. Reptiles need to be warm to hunt and digest their food.

Cooling off
A crocodile cools down by 'gaping' its mouth very wide. Or, it can take a dip in the river or lie in the shade.

Reptile skin

All animals need skin to keep their insides in and to stop them drying out in the sun. Skin also helps to protect the animal's insides from injury.

Spiky skin

Some reptiles, such as iguanas, have spikes down their backs to protect them from predators. These tough scales are made of keratin.

predators – animals that hunt other animals

Smooth skin

Burrowing reptiles such as sandfish have smooth, flexible scales. These lie flat against the skin to help the animal slide into its burrow.

Growing bigger

A snake sheds its skin as it grows. It wriggles until it is free of the old skin. This is called sloughing.

keratin – a tough, horny substance found in hair, claws and fingernails

Reptile senses

Senses help animals understand their world. All animals use their senses to find food, keep safe and find a mate. Most reptiles can see, hear and smell, and some can 'taste' things in the air.

eardrum

Listening lizards
Lizards do not have soft ears on the outside of the head like we do. They have an eardrum on each side of their head to pick up sounds.

eardrum – a part of the ear that sends sound vibrations to the inner ear

Tasting smells

Many snakes and lizards flick
out their tongue to 'taste' the
air. A sense organ in the mouth
works out what the tastes are.

Looking all around

A chameleon can move
each eye on its own.
This means the animal
can look in two different
directions at one time.

organ – a part of the body with a special job

Foot functions

Reptiles exist all over the world, so they live in many different habitats. Their feet have evolved and adapted to suit their way of living. Some climb, some dig, while others can grip on to branches.

Spreading the weight

Giant tortoises have huge feet. As they clamber over sandy ground, their big feet help to spread out their weight so that they do not sink.

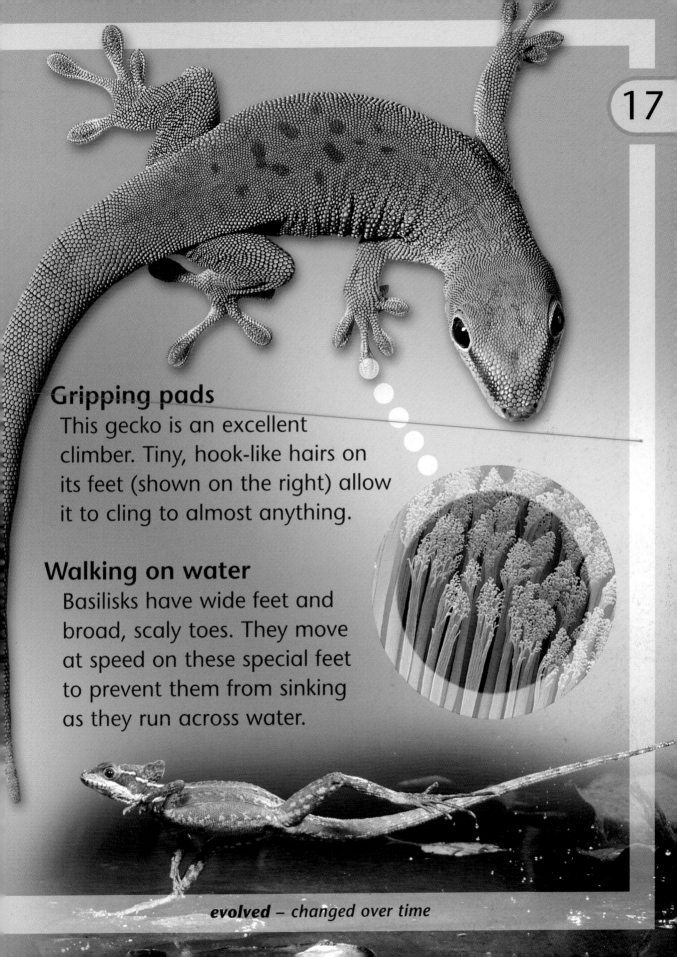

Gripping pads

This gecko is an excellent climber. Tiny, hook-like hairs on its feet (shown on the right) allow it to cling to almost anything.

Walking on water

Basilisks have wide feet and broad, scaly toes. They move at speed on these special feet to prevent them from sinking as they run across water.

evolved – changed over time

Fangs and teeth

Some reptiles are small and hunt insects. Larger ones eat meatier creatures such as mammals. All reptiles have a mouth and teeth suited to catching and eating their prey.

Snapping jaws

Alligator snapping turtles have sharp edges to their strong jaws. They snap them shut to slice prey into bite-size pieces.

mammals – warm-blooded animals that feed their young on milk

Fold-away fangs

This rattlesnake has two sharp,
hollow teeth called fangs, which
unfold for biting. Poison is pumped
through the fangs to kill the prey.

Catching fish

The mouth of the Ganges gharial
is lined with small, sharp teeth.
The teeth fit together tightly to
stop fish from getting away.

prey – *an animal hunted by another animal*

Moving on land

All reptiles have a bony skeleton that helps to give their body its shape. Many have four legs, but snakes and some lizards do not have any legs. Most reptiles can move quickly to hunt or escape from danger.

Handling the heat

The Namib sand gecko has long legs. When it gets too hot, the gecko pushes up on these legs to lift its belly clear of the scorching desert sands.

flexible – *bendy, stretchy*

Sidewinding

Sidewinder rattlesnakes wriggle and loop their body along the hot ground. This way, only a small part of the body touches the baking hot sand at any one time.

Inside a snake

A snake's skeleton has a flexible backbone with ribs attached. It is very bendy, so a snake can coil up or wrap around things.

coil – to wind round and round in loops

Moving in water

Some reptiles live in water, while others swim to find food or to cool themselves down. All reptiles breathe air, so even those living in water have to surface from time to time to take in air.

Finding food

Marine iguanas are the world's only ocean lizards. They feed on seaweed and can stay underwater for about 20 minutes.

Graceful swimmers

Green sea turtles beat their front flippers like wings and use their back ones to steer. Their smooth shells help them to move in water.

Powerful swimmers

Saltwater crocodiles swish their long tails from side to side to push them through water. Their legs help them to steer.

flippers – limbs that are suited to swimming

Moving in trees

Many reptiles are good at climbing. Tree-living geckos have special foot pads for gripping slippery leaves, while some snakes have ridged scales for clinging to branches.

Clinging on

Tree snakes have long, strong bodies. They wrap themselves around branches and reach out into the open to look for predators or prey.

glide – to float gently through the air

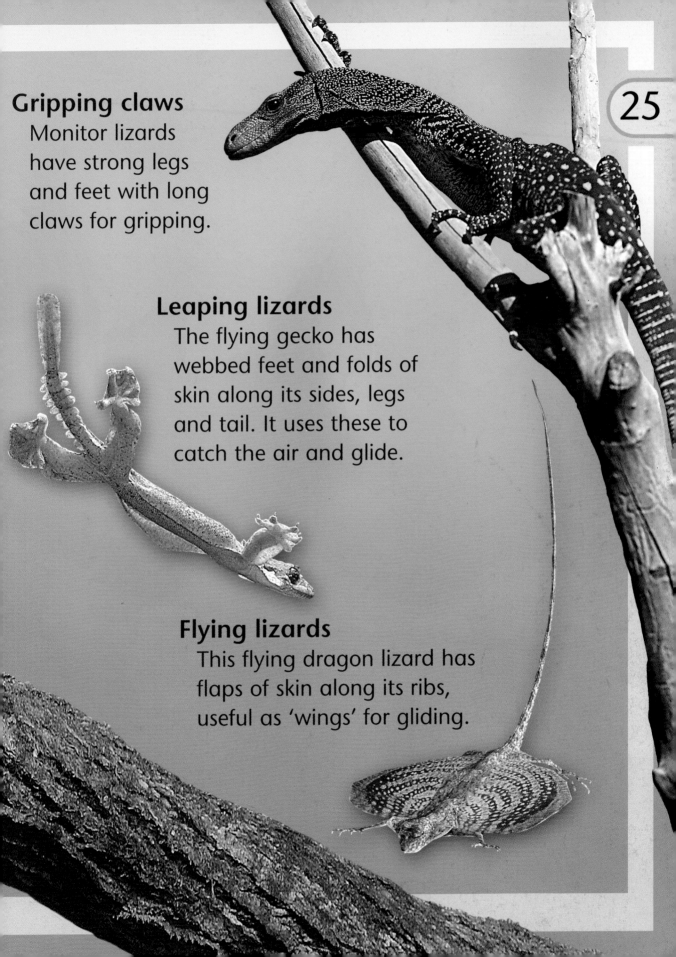

Gripping claws

Monitor lizards have strong legs and feet with long claws for gripping.

Leaping lizards

The flying gecko has webbed feet and folds of skin along its sides, legs and tail. It uses these to catch the air and glide.

Flying lizards

This flying dragon lizard has flaps of skin along its ribs, useful as 'wings' for gliding.

Finding food

Although some lizards eat only plants, most reptiles are carnivores that hunt other animals. Some reptiles, such as crocodiles, have a varied diet, while others eat just one type of food.

Elastic tongue
Chameleons grip on to branches. They have a long, sticky tongue, which they shoot out at high speed to catch any bugs they see.

carnivores – animals that eat meat

Eating frogs' eggs

When the cat-eyed snake finds a cluster of frogs' eggs, it slurps up the whole sticky mass.

Leafy dinner

The Solomon island skink is strictly a plant-eater. It climbs trees to feast on the fresh green leaves.

Fresh eggs

The African egg-eating snake swallows eggs whole. It pierces the shells in its throat, so as not to spill what is inside.

pierce – to prick and break into

Finding a mate

When animals are ready to breed, they find a mate. Some reptiles use smell to attract a partner, while others use colours, sounds and even dancing. Many males fight to win the female.

Bright throat

This male anole lizard puffs up its colourful throat and nods its head up and down. This shows females he is ready to mate and warns off rival males.

breed – *to produce babies*

Breeding dance
Speckled rattlesnake males prove their strength by wrestling. They are venomous, but they do not bite each other.

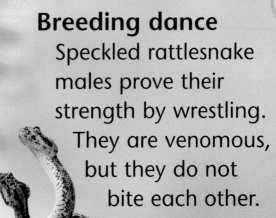

Wrestling match
Using their tails for support, male monitors rear up on their back legs and fight rival males. The weaker male gives up.

venomous – poisonous

Reptile eggs

Most reptiles lay eggs with soft yet tough shells. The egg's yolk provides the developing young with food. The shell protects it from outside conditions.

developing – *growing and changing*

A turtle nest

This Olive Ridley sea turtle is laying about 100 eggs into a hole she has dug in the sand. She will return to the sea after burying them.

Breaking out

Developing snakes grow an 'egg tooth' on the tip of their upper jaw. They use this to pierce the egg's shell when they are ready to hatch.

Live babies

Some snakes and lizards give birth to live young. This lizard's Arctic home is too cold for eggs.

hatch – to break out of an egg

Growing up

Baby reptiles usually look like small versions of the adults. They are able to catch their own food as soon as they hatch. Some begin by eating smaller prey than the adults eat.

Digging for freedom
Newly hatched Olive Ridley sea turtles dig their way out of their sandy nests. They crawl as quickly as they can towards the sea.

miniature – tiny

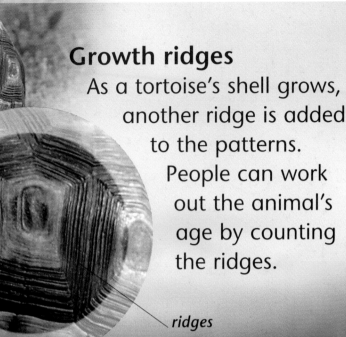

Growth ridges

As a tortoise's shell grows, another ridge is added to the patterns. People can work out the animal's age by counting the ridges.

ridges

Caring mothers

Although a fierce predator, this female Nile crocodile is a caring mother. She gently scoops her babies into her mouth to keep them safe.

ridge – a narrow, raised area on a flat surface

Keeping safe

Reptiles use many different tricks to stay hidden while out hunting or while resting. If startled, some pretend to be dead. Others show that they are poisonous by being brightly coloured.

Armour plating

An armadillo lizard has sharp, spiny growths on its skin. When threatened, the lizard grabs its tail and curls up into a spiky ball.

startled – surprised

Hiding in leaves

Gaboon vipers have mottled patterns on their skin. This helps them stay hidden among leaf-litter.

Gaboon viper

Too big to eat?

Frilled lizards have a flap of skin around their heads that they can raise up. This makes them look bigger and scarier if a predator attacks.

mottled – *patterned with different coloured patches*

Dragons and devils

Lizards are the most successful group of reptiles and live in many different places. Some have developed into big and fierce predators. Others are much smaller and live in trees, or even underground.

Dragons with beards

When threatened, the bearded dragon puffs up a spiky flap of skin under its chin. This makes it look too big to eat.

Big dragons

Komodo dragons are the largest of all lizards. They can catch goats and pigs, but usually they eat carrion.

carrion – the dead bodies of animals

Thorny devils

A thorny devil's spines and prickles protect the animal from attack. They also catch dew for the lizard to drink.

dew – *small drops of water that form in the night on grass and plants*

Using poisons

Many reptiles use venom (poison) to kill prey. Venom can affect the nervous system, the tissues of the body or even blood. Venomous reptiles may also use these poisons for self-defence.

Spitting cobras

A spitting cobra sprays venom out of its mouth. It aims for its enemy's eyes. The poison is very painful and can cause blindness.

nervous system – *the network of nerves throughout an animal's body*

A poisonous bite

Gila monsters are one
of two venomous lizard
species. Their venomous
saliva (spit) poisons prey
as they bite and chew.

Swimming snakes

Sea snakes are the most
venomous snakes in the
world. They can swim
underwater for up
to five hours.

Noisy rattles

Rattlesnakes twitch the
loose scales at the end
of their tail to make a
rattling sound. This
warns that their
bite is poisonous.

saliva – clear liquid produced in the mouth

A future for reptiles

Many reptiles are in danger or face becoming extinct. We must learn how our actions may harm reptiles, and do more to look after them.

Harmful trade

Many reptiles are killed for their skins. The skins are then used to make wallets, boots and belts, or souvenirs for tourists.

Tracking reptiles

This loggerhead turtle is being fitted with a radio transmitter. Scientists will monitor its movements so that they can learn more about this creature.

extinct – *when all animals of a certain type die, and none are left*

Returning to the wild
This alligator was once caught and sold as a pet. Luckily, it was rescued and returned to its real home.

radio transmitter – *a device that sends out signals that can be tracked*

Lizard cape

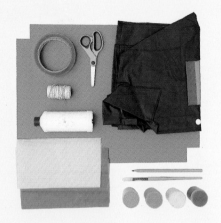

Make your own frilled cape

The Australian frilled lizard defends itself using its neck frill (see page 35). Make one yourself to see how this special defensive system works.

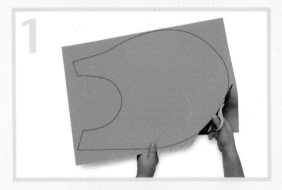

Draw one half of the frill shape on to a large sheet of coloured card. Use scissors to cut out the shape.

You will need

- Two large sheets of card
- Pencil
- Scissors
- Sticky tape
- Poster paints
- Paint brush
- Coloured tissue paper
- Glue
- String

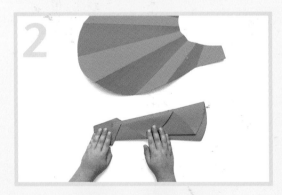

Make the other half of the frill with another sheet of card. Fold each half like a concertina.

Place the two halves together and join them using sticky tape at one end.

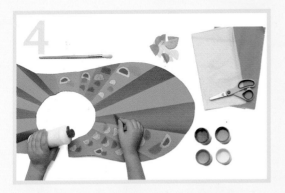

Create a pattern for your cape using paint. Cut out pieces of tissue paper and stick on using glue to create a scaly texture.

Cut two long pieces of string. Attach them at either end of the cape – to the unpainted side – using sticky tape.

Place the finished cape around your neck and use the string to hold it in position. Give it a tug to raise the frilly cape and scare off your enemies!

Pop-up croc

Create a greetings card
Learn how to cut and fold paper to make your very own pop-up card. Then decorate it for a friend or relative.

You will need
- Coloured card
- Pencil
- Scissors
- Poster paints and brush

1 Fold the card in half and draw a zig-zag line for the croc's teeth. Cut along the line using scissors.

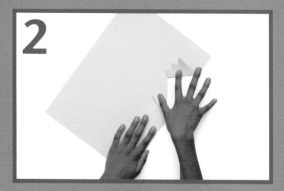

2 Fold the teeth shape out as shown, so that there is a definite crease. Unfold the card so that it lies flat.

3 Draw out the rest of your croc in pencil and colour it with paints. Press out the teeth to make the card work.

Snake stick

Make a slinky snake toy

Snakes have a flexible backbone. Create this model, then use the stick to copy the way a snake coils and slinks over land.

Use a ruler to draw out equal strips on the coloured card. Use scissors to cut out the strips.

You will need
- Coloured card
- Pencil
- Ruler
- Scissors
- Sticky tape
- Paints
- Paint brush
- String
- Wooden cane

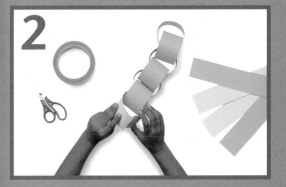

Using sticky tape, make one strip into a loop. Join other strips on in loops. Add a pointed loop for tail.

Add eyes and a forked tongue. Paint markings on. Stick one end of string near head, and other end to a cane.

Sticky tongues

Play at being a chameleon

Chameleons shoot out their sticky tongues to snatch up juicy bugs (see page 26). With this fun game, you can pretend to do the same!

1

Roll up sheets of card to make two tubes – one slightly thinner. Fasten tubes using tape. Paint tubes red.

You will need
- Coloured card
- Sticky tape
- Poster paints
- Paint brush
- Red tissue paper
- Double-sided sticky tape
- Black tissue paper
- White tissue paper
- Scissors

2

Slot the slightly thinner tube inside the larger one. Use sticky tape to hold the two tubes together.

3

Screw up lots of red tissue paper into a ball. Add strips of double-sided tape to make it sticky.

4

Push the ball of tissue into the end of the long tube. The double-sided tape should hold it in. This forms the tip of your sticky tongue.

5

Make flies by screwing up smaller pieces of black tissue paper. Cut out wing shapes using white paper or tissue. Stick them on using tape.

Make two of these sticky tongues. Then, put all your flies into a bowl, or on a paper plate, and you are ready to play... The person who collects the most flies in one minute is the winning chameleon!

Index